This Journal Belongs To

_____

Visit Us At
www.ascendprints.com

Copyright © 2020
Ascend Prints

For details and to order more copies, please visit AscendPrints.com

All rights reserved. No part of this publication may be reproduced or transmitted in any form or by any means, without first seeking permission from the publisher.

God is Calling You...

Hi there,

You have found this journal and it's designed to help you bring yourself closer to God. This is meant to help record your thoughts and prayers for your time in prayer and fasting. Your prayers changes things and God is waiting to hear your faith-filled words. May the pages of this book help you with your relationship with God and may it help you make an impact with people, your community, and the world.

Be strong AND courageous

JOSHUA 1:9

How to Use This Journal

Daily Schedule

Schedule your day daily to map out your spiritual journey.
You can customize your own schedule to help you track your days.

I'm Thankful

Studies shows that thankfulness can increase your mood and happiness.
You can write what you are grateful for and express your gratitude to the Lord.

Bible Verses

Beautifully designed for you to share what scriptures are on your heart.
The Bible is designed to help you with your prayer and fasting.

Prayer

Plenty of room for you to pray to God and what you would like to express to Him.
You can write out your prayers or write down what God has been saying to you.

THE JOY OF THE LORD IS YOUR *Strength*

NEHEMIAH 8:10

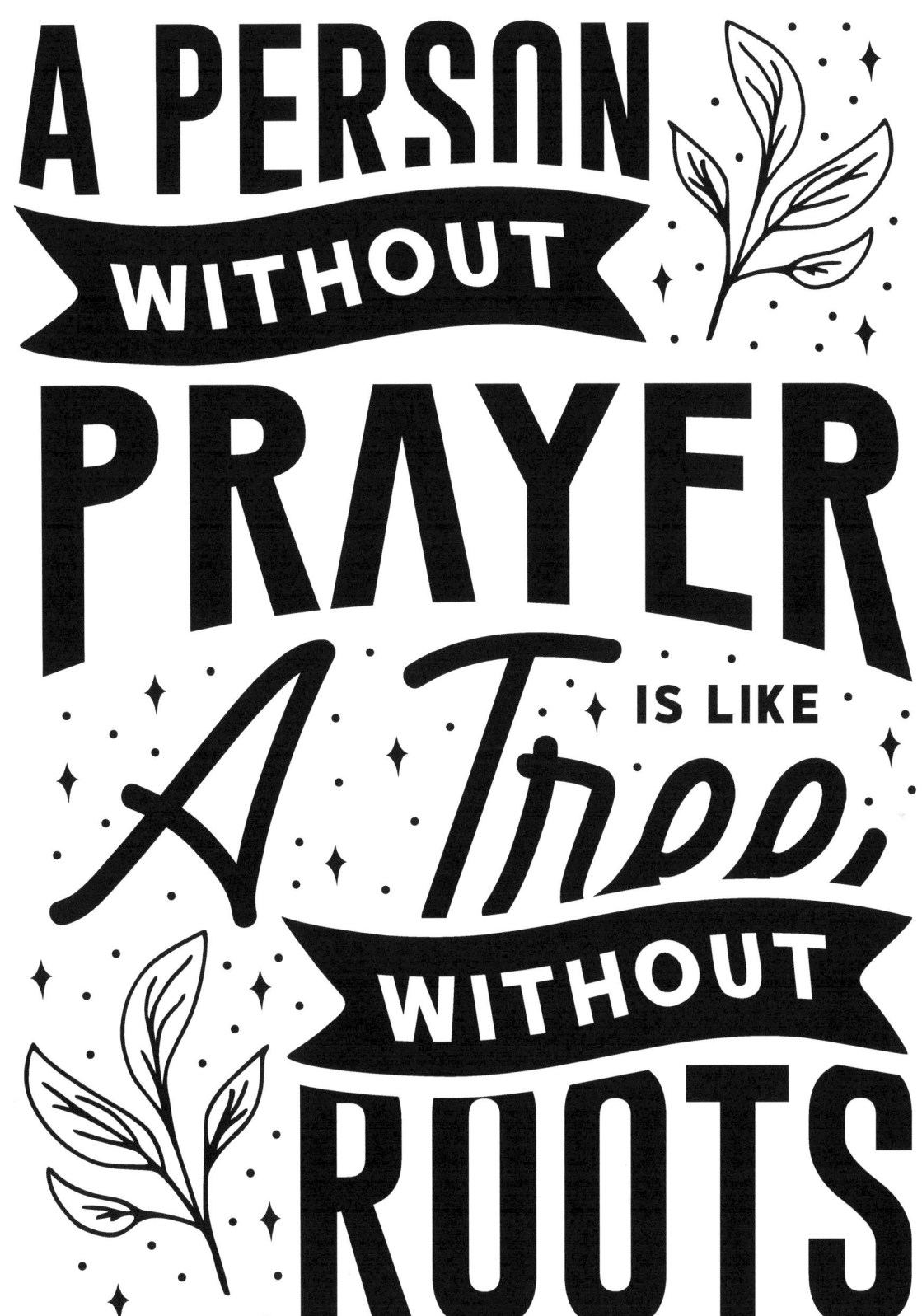

Day 1 of Fasting and Prayer

DAILY SCHEDULE

5
6
7
8
9
10
11
12
1
2
3
4
5
6
7
8

I'M THANKFUL

BIBLE VERSES

PRAYER

In prayer there is healing and restoration

Blessed ♡ Are Those ♡ Who Teach

Day 2 of Fasting and Prayer

DAILY SCHEDULE

5
6
7
8
9
10
11
12
1
2
3
4
5
6
7
8

I'M THANKFUL

BIBLE VERSES

PRAYER

But First Pray

Can I Get An Amen #Believer

Day 3 of Fasting and Prayer

DAILY SCHEDULE

5
6
7
8
9
10
11
12
1
2
3
4
5
6
7
8

I'M THANKFUL

BIBLE VERSES

PRAYER

Choose Joy Romans 15:13

Faith Before Fear

Day 4 of Fasting and Prayer

DAILY SCHEDULE

5
6
7
8
9
10
11
12
1
2
3
4
5
6
7
8

I'M THANKFUL

BIBLE VERSES

PRAYER

Faith Hope Love

Faith Over Fear

Day 5 of Fasting and Prayer

DAILY SCHEDULE

5
6
7
8
9
10
11
12
1
2
3
4
5
6
7
8

I'M THANKFUL

BIBLE VERSES

PRAYER

PRAY BY faith

God Is Great Always

Day 6 of Fasting and Prayer

DAILY SCHEDULE

5
6
7
8
9
10
11
12
1
2
3
4
5
6
7
8

I'M THANKFUL

BIBLE VERSES

PRAYER

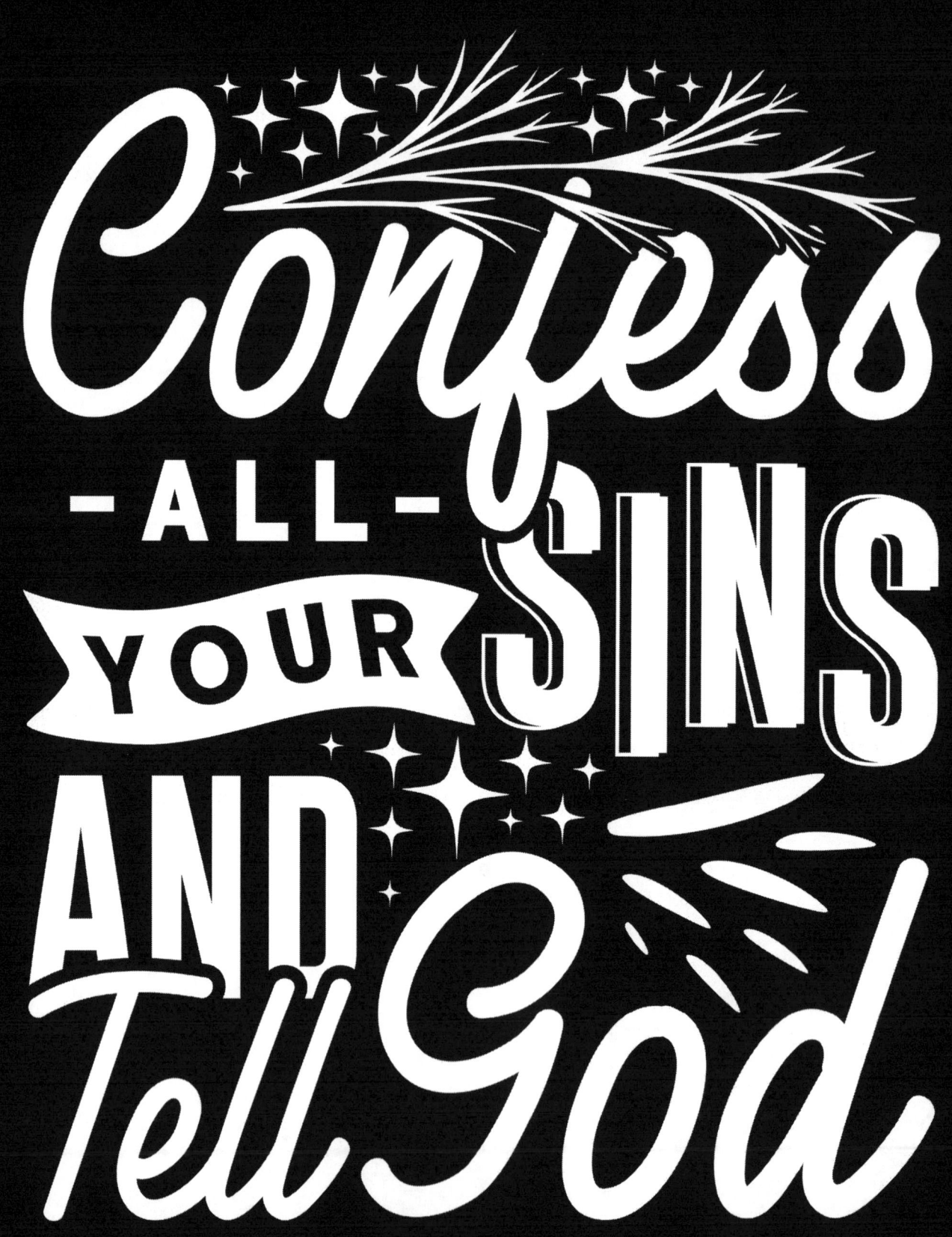

Day 7 of Fasting and Prayer

DAILY SCHEDULE

5
6
7
8
9
10
11
12
1
2
3
4
5
6
7
8

I'M THANKFUL

BIBLE VERSES

PRAYER

The Prayer of the Righteous is Powerful

You Can Bring Everything To Him In Prayer

Day 8 of Fasting and Prayer

DAILY SCHEDULE

5
6
7
8
9
10
11
12
1
2
3
4
5
6
7
8

I'M THANKFUL

BIBLE VERSES

PRAYER

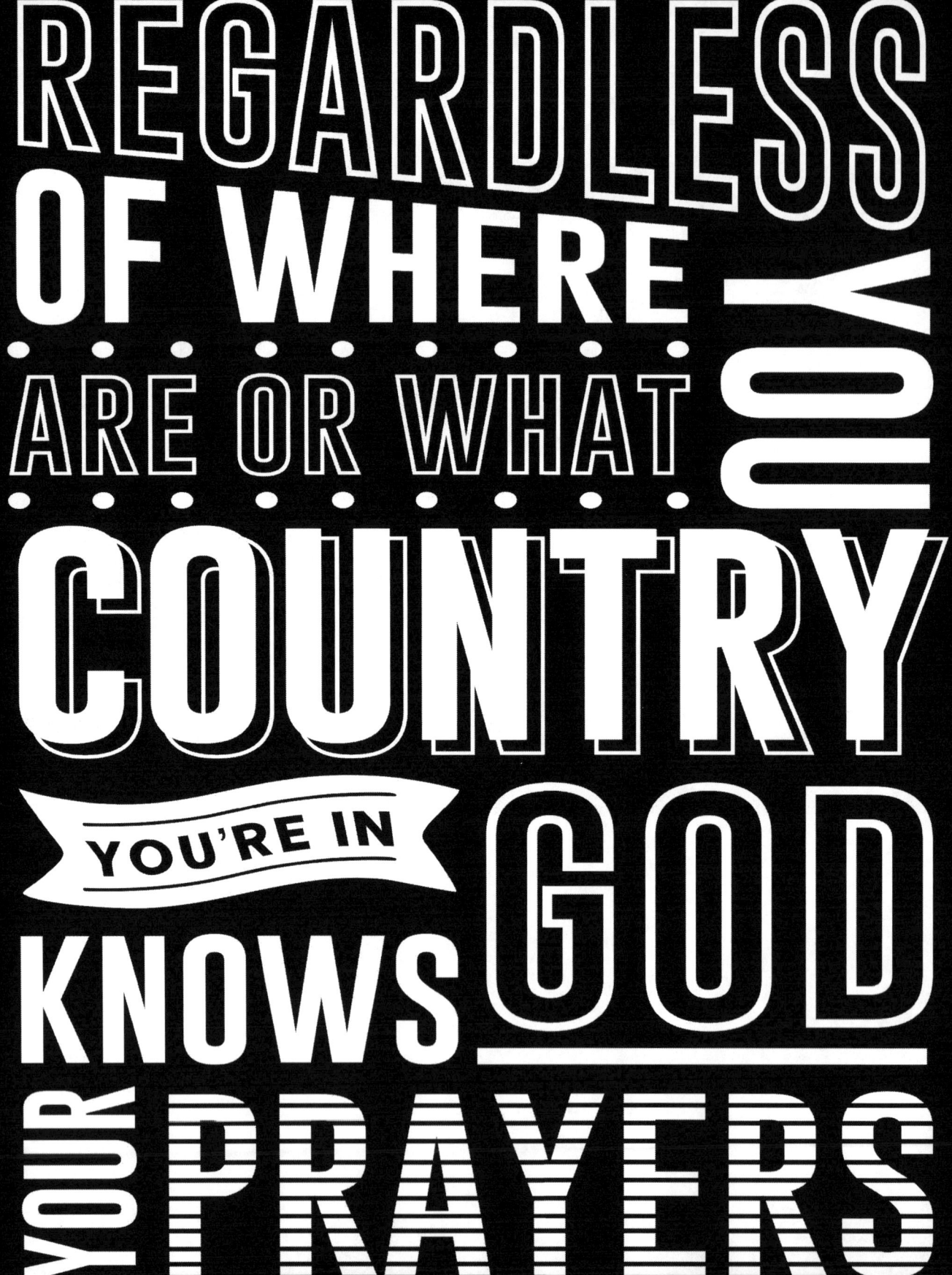

REGARDLESS OF WHERE YOU ARE OR WHAT COUNTRY YOU'RE IN GOD KNOWS YOUR PRAYERS

He Left The 99 Rescue me

Day 9 of Fasting and Prayer

DAILY SCHEDULE

5
6
7
8
9
10
11
12
1
2
3
4
5
6
7
8

I'M THANKFUL

BIBLE VERSES

PRAYER

I Am Chosen

Jesus Loves Me

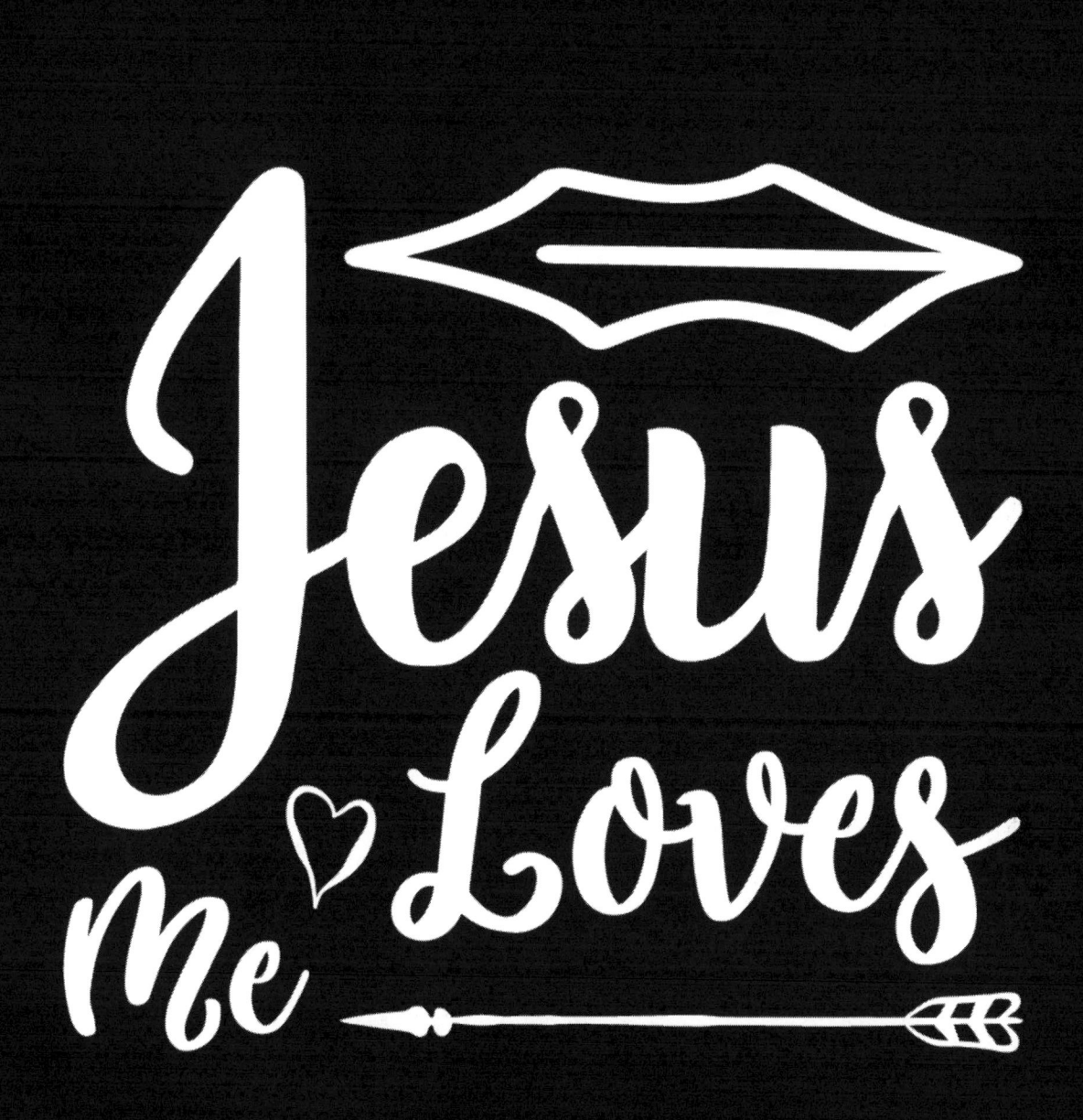

Day 10 of Fasting and Prayer

DAILY SCHEDULE

5
6
7
8
9
10
11
12
1
2
3
4
5
6
7
8

I'M THANKFUL

BIBLE VERSES

PRAYER

Love Never Fails

Corinthians 13:8

Loved
John 3:16

Day 11 of Fasting and Prayer

DAILY SCHEDULE

5
6
7
8
9
10
11
12
1
2
3
4
5
6
7
8

I'M THANKFUL

BIBLE VERSES

PRAYER

Not Perfect Just Forgiven

Not Today Satan

Day 12 of Fasting and Prayer

DAILY SCHEDULE

5
6
7
8
9
10
11
12
1
2
3
4
5
6
7
8

I'M THANKFUL

BIBLE VERSES

PRAYER

Pray Big

Rejoice In The Lord

Day 13 of Fasting and Prayer

DAILY SCHEDULE

5
6
7
8
9
10
11
12
1
2
3
4
5
6
7
8

I'M THANKFUL

BIBLE VERSES

PRAYER

Rise Up & Pray
Luke 22:46

Strong Brave Fearless
JOSHUA 1:9

Day 14 of Fasting and Prayer

DAILY SCHEDULE

5
6
7
8
9
10
11
12
1
2
3
4
5
6
7
8

I'M THANKFUL

BIBLE VERSES

PRAYER

Walk By Faith Not Sight

I'M FEARFULLY ✝ ✝ and WONDERFULLY MADE

Day 15 of Fasting and Prayer

DAILY SCHEDULE

5
6
7
8
9
10
11
12
1
2
3
4
5
6
7
8

I'M THANKFUL

BIBLE VERSES

PRAYER

Faith over fear

grow in grace

Day 16 of Fasting and Prayer

DAILY SCHEDULE

5
6
7
8
9
10
11
12
1
2
3
4
5
6
7
8

I'M THANKFUL

BIBLE VERSES

PRAYER

Jesus Over Everything

The Lord will guide You always

Isaiah 58:11

Day 17 of Fasting and Prayer

DAILY SCHEDULE

5
6
7
8
9
10
11
12
1
2
3
4
5
6
7
8

I'M THANKFUL

BIBLE VERSES

PRAYER

THE LORD

Will Be Your

EVERLASTING LIGHT

isaiah 60:20

...she is...
Strong
proverbs 31:25

Day 18 of Fasting and Prayer

DAILY SCHEDULE

5
6
7
8
9
10
11
12
1
2
3
4
5
6
7
8

I'M THANKFUL

BIBLE VERSES

PRAYER

Rise up

TAKE COURAGE

and do it.

EZRA 10:4

Our Faith Can Move Mountains

Matthew 17:20

Day 19 of Fasting and Prayer

DAILY SCHEDULE

5
6
7
8
9
10
11
12
1
2
3
4
5
6
7
8

I'M THANKFUL

BIBLE VERSES

PRAYER

Nothing is IMPOSSIBLE with God

LUKE 1:37

Love one another

john 13:34

Day 20 of Fasting and Prayer

DAILY SCHEDULE

5
6
7
8
9
10
11
12
1
2
3
4
5
6
7
8

I'M THANKFUL

BIBLE VERSES

PRAYER

LORD
LET THEM SEE YOU IN
me

Joy Comes ...in the... Morning

psalm 30:5

Day 21 of Fasting and Prayer

DAILY SCHEDULE

5
6
7
8
9
10
11
12
1
2
3
4
5
6
7
8

I'M THANKFUL

BIBLE VERSES

PRAYER

I WILL NOT BE *Shaken*

— PSALM 16:8

I Trust in the Lord

Thank You for using this journal

BUY PRINTABLES & DIGITAL PLANNERS

Shop now at AscendPrints.com

You will find all of our printable planner, trackers, to-do lists, and many more at our shop. Buy one today and get it instantly to your email as a digital download today!

GET YOUR FREE PRINTABLE DIGITAL DOWNLOAD

Check out our shop at AscendPrints.com to find your free printable for an instant download.

DID YOU LIKE OUR PRODUCT? LEAVE A REVIEW

Show your support for Ascend Prints and help other journal and planner users discover our products. Find this book on Amazon and scroll to the reviews section and click, "Write a customer review." We read every review, so thank you for taking the time to review our product.

Made in the USA
Columbia, SC
23 September 2023